1001 Great Inspirational Quotes
- find the perfect quote you need

Peter V.G. Kristiansen

1001 Great Inspirational Quotes

For Peter Leth Møller
Dear friend and great inspiration

Content

Great quotes on Success

Along with success comes a reputation for wisdom.
Euripides

They can because they think they can.
Virgil

Nothing can stop the man with the right mental attitude from achieving his goal; nothing on earth can help the man with the wrong mental attitude.
Thomas Jefferson

Keep steadily before you the fact that all true success depends at last upon yourself.
Theodore T. Hunger

We are all motivated by a keen desire for praise, and the better a man is, the more he is inspired to glory.
Cicero

There are three kinds of people in the world, the wills, the won'ts and the can'ts. The first accomplish everything; the second oppose everything; the third fail in everything.

The thing always happens that you really believe in; and the belief in a thing makes it happen.
Frank Loyd Wright

The surest way not to fail is to determine to succeed.
Richard Brinsley Sheridan

A failure is a man who has blundered, but is not able to cash in on the experience.
Elbert Hubbard

There is only one success - to be able to spend your life in your own way.
Christopher Morley

Success is sweet: the sweeter if long delayed and attained through manifold struggles and defeats.
A. Branson Alcott

The secret of success is to know something nobody else knows.
Aristotle Onassis

The greatest results in life are usually attained by simple means and the exercise of ordinary qualities. These may for the most part be summed in these two: common sense and perseverance.
Owen Feltham

Failures do what is tension relieving, while winners do what is goal achieving.
Dennis Waitley

The difference between a successful person and others is not a lack of strength, not a lack of knowledge, but rather a lack in will.
Vince Lombardi

Everyone has a fair turn to be as great as he pleases.
Jeremy Collier

Success does not consist in never making blunders, but in never making the same one the second time.
H. W. Shaw

There is always room at the top.
Daniel Webster

There is no royal road to anything. One thing at a time, all things in succession. That which grows fast, withers as rapidly. That which grows slowly, endures.
Josiah Gilbert Holland

The great thing in this world is not so much where you stand, as in what direction you are moving.
Oliver Wendell Holmes

It is not enough to aim, you must hit.
Italian Proverb

There is only one success – to be able to spend your life in your own way.
Christopher Morley

Either attempt it not, or succeed.
Ovid

I cannot give you the formula for success, but I can give you the formula for failure - which is: Try to please everybody.
Herbert Bayard Swope

Success does not consist in never making blunders, but in never making the same one a second time.
Josh Billings

It is with many enterprises as with striking fire; we do not meet with success except by reiterated efforts, and often at the instant when we despaired of success.
Francoise de Maintenon

The secret of success in life is for a man to be ready for his opportunity when it comes.
Earl of Beaconsfield

Success is the good fortune that comes from aspiration, desperation, perspiration and inspiration.
Evan Esar

If you wish success in life, make perseverance your bosom friend, experience your wise counselor, caution your elder brother, and hope your guardian genius.
Jospeph Addison

Impatience never commanded success.
Edwin H. Chapin

The talent of success is nothing more than doing what you can do, well.
Henry W. Longfellow

To climb steep hills requires a slow pace at first.
William Shakespeare

Try not to become a man of success but a man of value.
Albert Einstein

The man who makes a success of an important venture never wails for the crowd. He strikes out for himself. It takes nerve, it takes a great lot of grit; but the man that succeeds has both. Anyone can fail. The public admires the man who has enough confidence in himself to take a chance. These chances are the main things after all. The man who tries to succeed must expect to be criticized. Nothing important was ever done but the greater number consulted previously doubted the possibility. Success is the accomplishment of that which most people think can't be done.
C. V. White

If at first you don't succeed, try, try again. Then quit. There's no use being a damn fool about it.
W.C. Fields

Success is the sum of small efforts, repeated day in and day out.
Robert Collier

Great Quotes on Life

Dost thou love life?
Then do not squander time,
for that is the stuff life is made of.
Benjamin Franklin

Life is either a daring adventure or nothing.
Helen Keller

Life is like a game of cards. The hand that is dealt you represents
determinism; the way you play it is free will.
Jawaharal Nehru

Life is like the dice that, falling, still show a different face. So life,
though it remains the same, is always presenting different
aspects.
Alexis

Our life's a stage, a comedy: either learn to play and take it
lightly, or bear its troubles patiently.
Palladas

The geat blessing of mankind are within us and within our reach;
but we shut our eyes, and like people in the dark, we fall foul
upon the very thing we search for, without finding it.
Seneca
(7 B.C. - 65 A.D.)

Govern thy life and thoughts as if the whole world were to see
the one, and read the other.
Thomas Fuller

Dance as though no one is watching you.
Love as though you have never been hurt before
Sing as though no one can hear you
Live as though heaven is on Earth
Souza

Most of the shadows of this life are caused by our standing in our own sunshine.
Ralph Waldo Emerson

Life, in all ranks and situations, is an outward occupation, an actual and active work.
W. Humboldt

The unexamined life is not worth living.
Socrates

Unrest of spirit is a mark of life; one problem after another presents itself and in the solving of them we can find our greatest pleasure.
Kal Menninger

Life is short, art long, opportunity fleeting, experience treacherous,
judgment difficult.
Hypocrites

After the game,
the king and the pawn go into the same box.
Italian Proverb

The acts of this life are the destiny of the next.
Eastern Proverb

Life is a tragedy for those who feel, and a comedy for those who think.
La Bruyere

Life is like a library owned by the author.
In it are a few books which he wrote himself,
but most of them were written for him.
Harry Emerson Fosdick

We make our fortunes, and we call them fate.
Earl of Beaconsfield

The best way to prepare for life is to begin to live.
Elbert Hubbard

Life's a voyage that's homeward bound.
Herman Melville

The whole of life is but a moment of time. It is our duty,
therefore to use it, not to misuse it.
Plutarch

Life is variable.
Plautus

Life is a rich strain of music, suggesting a realm too fair to be.
George William Curtis

I made my life my monument.
Ben Johnson

The boundaries, which divide life from death
are at best shadowy and vague.
Who shall say where one ends,
and the other begins?
Edgar Alan Poe

One way to get the most out of life is
to look upon it as an adventure.
William Feather

Life without endeavor is like entering a jewel mine and coming
out with empty hands.
Japanese Proverb

Life is a succession of lessons, which must be lived to be
understood.
Ralph Waldo Emerson

There are no classes in life for beginners: right away you are
always asked to deal with what is most difficult.
Rainer Maria Rilke

To live is like to love - all reason is against it, and all healthy
instinct for it.
Samuel Butler

One life - a little gleam of time between two eternities.
Thomas Carlyle

Life is a pure flame,
and we live by an invisible sun within us.
Sir Thomas Brown

As I grow to understand life less and less,
I learn to love it more and more.
Jules Renard

Great quotes on Inspiration

Try not to become a man of success but a man of value.
Albert Einstein

If you have built castles in the air, your work need not be lost;
that is where they should be. Now put foundations under them.
Henry David Thoreau

Inspiration and genius: one and the same.
Victor Hugo

To find what you seek in the road of life,
the best proverb of all is that which says:
"Leave no stone unturned."
Edward Bulwer Lytton

If you would create something,
you must be something.
Johann Wolfgang von Goethe

Every artist was first an amateur.
Ralph Waldo Emerson

The more difficulties one has to encounter, within and without,
the more significant and the higher in inspiration his life will be.
Horace Bushnell

Life has no smooth road for any of us; and in the bracing
atmosphere of a high aim the very roughness stimulates the
climber to steadier steps, till the legend, over steep ways to the
stars, fulfils itself.
W. C. Doane

Experience is the child of thought, and thought is the child of
action.
Benjamin Disraeli

Do we not all agree to call rapid thought and noble impulse by the name of inspiration?
George Eliot

Patience and the mulberry leaf becomes a silk gown.
Chinese Proverb

Every generation laughs at the old fashions,
but religiously follows the new.
Henry David Thoreau

No great man ever complains of want of opportunities.
Ralph Waldo Emerson

Circumstances? I make circumstances!
Napoleon I

Men do less than they ought, unless they do all they can.
Thomas Carlyle

Let thy words be few.
Ecclesiastes 5:2 from Words of Wisdom

Happy are those who dream dreams and are ready to pay the price to make them come true.
Leon J. Suenes

The power of imagination makes us infinite.
John Muir

Fall seven times, stand up eight.
Japanese proverb

First say to yourself what you would be;
and then do what you have to do.
Epictetus

The great blessings of mankind are within us, and within our reach; but we shut our eyes, and, like people in the dark, we fall foul upon the very thing we search for, without finding it.
Seneca

You miss 100% of the shots you don't take.
Wayne Gretzky

Great quotes on Motivation

It was a high counsel that I once heard given to a young person,
"Always do what you are afraid to do."
Ralph Waldo Emerson

Take calculated risks.
That is quite different from being rash.
George S. Patton

Storms make oaks take roots.
Proverb

If you do not hope, you will not find what is beyond your hopes.
St. Clement of Alexandra

We are all inventors, each sailing out on a voyage of discovery,
guided each by a private chart, of which there is no duplicate.
The world is all gates, all opportunities.
Ralph Waldo Emerson

Seek the lofty by reading, hearing and seeing great work at some
moment every day.
Thornton Wilder

The only way of finding the limits of the possible is by going
beyond them into the impossible.
Arthur C. Clarke

Play for more than you can afford to
lose and you will learn the game.
Winston Churchill

Without inspiration the best powers of the mind remain
dormant. There is a fuel in us which needs to be ignited with
sparks.
Johann Gottfried Von Herder

And all may do what has by man been done.
Edward Young

We are what we repeatedly do. Excellence, therefore, is not an
act but a habit.
Aristotle

Hope is like the sun, which, as we journey toward it, casts the
shadow of our burden behind us.
Samuel Smiles

Work spares us from three evils: boredom, vice, and need.
Voltaire

If the wind will not serve,
take to the oars.
Destitutus ventis, remos adhibe
Latin Proverb

Men's best successes come after their disappointments.
Henry Ward Beecher

You cannot plough a field by
turning it over in your mind.
Author Unknown

The best way out is always through.
Robert Frost

Do not wait to strike till the iron is hot; but make it hot by
striking.
William B. Sprague

Nothing will ever be attempted if all possible objections must
first be overcome.
Samuel Johnson

Fortune favors the brave.
Publius Terence

When the best things are not possible, the best may be made of those that are.
Richard Hooker

He who hesitates is lost.
Proverb

If you want to succeed in the world must make your own opportunities as you go on. The man who waits for some seventh wave to toss him on dry land will find that the seventh wave is a long time a coming. You can commit no greater folly than to sit by the roadside until some one comes along and invites you to ride with him to wealth or influence.
John B. Gough

Great spirits have always encountered violent opposition from mediocre minds.
Albert Einstein

Believe with all of your heart that you will do what you were made to do.
Orison Swett Marden

Take heed: you do not find what you do not seek.
English Proverb

Knowing is not enough; we must apply.
Willing is not enough; we must do.
Johann Wolfgang von Goethe

We are still masters of our fate.
We are still captains of our souls.
Winston Churchill

Nothing great was ever achieved without enthusiasm.
Ralph Waldo Emerson

For hope is but the dream
of those that wake.
Matthew Prior

Constant dripping hollows out a stone.
Lucretius

Nothing contributes so much to tranquilize the mind as a steady
purpose - a point on which the soul may fix its intellectual eye.
Mary Shelley

Heaven ne'er helps the man who will not help himself.
Sophocles

The journey of a thousand miles begins with a single step.
Lao Tzu

Industry is the parent of success.
Spanish Proverb

Thought is the seed of action.
Ralph Waldo Emerson

What lies behind us and what lies before us are tiny matters
compared to what lies within us.
Ralph Waldo Emerson
Self-trust is the first secret of success.
Ralph Waldo Emerson

When it is dark enough, you can see the stars.
Persian Proverb

You must know for which harbor you are headed if you are to
catch the right wind to take you there.
Seneca

Lots of things that couldn't be done have been done.
Charles Auston Bates

The winds and the waves are always on the side of the ablest navigators.
Edward Gibbon

They can conquer who believe they can.
Ralph Waldo Emerson

There are glimpses of heaven to us in every act, or thought, or word that raises us above ourselves.
A. P. Stanley

Be not afraid of greatness: some are born great, some achieve greatness, and some have greatness thrust upon them.
William Shakespeare

Great quotes on Wisdom

Nature and wisdom never are at strife.
Plutarch

It is easier to be wise for others than for ourselves.
Francois De La Rochefoucauld

The art of being wise is knowing what to overlook.
William James

The first step in the acquisition of wisdom is silence, the second
listening, the third memory, the fourth practice, the fifth teaching
others.
Solomon Ibn Gabriol

Years teach us more than books.
Berthold Auerbach

The wisdom of nations lies in their proverbs,
which are brief and pithy.
William Penn

The middle course is the best.
Cleobulus

The only medicine for suffering, crime, and all the other woes of
mankind, is wisdom.
Thomas Huxley

A wise man learns by the mistakes of others,
a fool by his own.
Latin Proverb

Silence does not always mark wisdom.
Samuel Taylor Coleridge.

No man was ever wise by chance.
Seneca

Not to know at large of things remote
From use, obscure and subtle, but to know
That which before us lies in daily life,
Is the prime wisdom.
John Milton

By associating with wise people you will become wise yourself.
Menander

The seat of knowledge is in the head, of wisdom,
in the heart.
William Hazlitt

Of all parts of wisdom the practice is the best.
John Tillotson

The more a man knows, the more he forgives.
Catherine the Great

A loving heart is the truest wisdom.
Charles Dickens

One who understands much displays a greater simplicity of
character than one who understands little.
Alexander Chase

How prone to doubt, how cautious are the wise!
Homer

It is easy to be wise after the event.
English Proverb

On every thorn, delightful wisdom grows,
In every rill a sweet instruction flows.
Edward Young

The man of wisdom is never of two minds;
the man of benevolence never worries;
the man of courage is never afraid.
Confucius

Great quotes on Happiness

When one door of happiness closes, another opens, but often we look so long at the closed door that we do not see the one that has been opened for us.
Helen Keller

Happiness does not consist in pastimes and amusements but in virtuous activities.
Aristotle

Happiness resides not in possessions and not in gold; the feeling of happiness dwells in the soul.
Democritus

The happiness of your life depends upon the quality of your thoughts; therefore guard accordingly.
Marcus Aurelius

People with many interests live, not only longest, but happiest.
George Matthew Allen

In the hopes of reaching the moon men fail to see the flowers that blossom at their feet.
Albert Schweitzer

Happiness is not achieved by the conscious pursuit of happiness; it is generally the by-product of other activities.
Aldous Huxley

One joy scatters a hundred grieves.
Chinese Proverb

There is only one person who could ever make you happy, and that person is you.
David Burns, Intimate Connections

The happiness of life is made up of minute fractions—the little soon-forgotten charities of a kiss, a smile, a kind look, a heartfelt compliment in the disguise of a playful raillery, and the countless other infinitesimals of pleasurable thought and genial feeling.
Samuel Taylor Coleridge

The man is happiest who lives from day to day and asks no more, garnering the simple goodness of life.
Euripides

Happiness consists in activity: such is the constitution of our nature; it is a running stream, and not a stagnant pool.
John M. Good

Happiness is not a state to arrive at, but a manner of traveling.
Margaret Lee Runbeck

A light heart lives long.
William Shakespeare

Men spend their lives in anticipations,—in determining to be vastly happy at some period when they have time. But the present time has one advantage over every other—it is our own. Past opportunities are gone, future have not come. We may lay in a stock of pleasures, as we would lay in a stock of wine; but if we defer the tasting of them too long, we shall find that both are soured by age.
Charles Caleb Colton

Who is the happiest of men? He who values the merits of others, and in their pleasure takes joy, even as though it was his own.
Johann Wolfgang von Goethe

The chances are that you have already come to believe that happiness is unattainable. But men have attained it. And they have attained it by realising that happiness does not spring from the procuring of physical or mental pleasure, but from the development of reason and the adjustment of conduct to principles.
- from How to Live on 24 Hours a Day, by Arnold Bennett

Happiness is not a matter of events; it depends upon the tides of the mind.
Alice Meynell

Fortify yourself with contentment, for this is an impregnable fortress.
Epictetus

Happiness does not depend on outward things, but on the way we see them.
Leo Tolstoy

Live each day as if your life had just begun.
Johann Wolfgang Von Goethe

Happiness depends more on the inward disposition of mind than on outward circumstances.
Benjamin Franklin

There is only one way to happiness, and that is to cease worrying things, which are beyond the power of our will.
Epictetus

I have learned to seek my happiness by limiting my desires, rather than attempting to satisfy them.
John Stuart Mills

You're happiest while you're making the greatest contribution.
Robert F. Kennedy

Action may not always bring happiness;
but there is no happiness without action.
Benjamin Disraeli

Great effort from great motives is the best definition of a happy
life.
William Ellery Channing

There is more to life than increasing its speed.
Mahatma Ghandi

The rays of happiness, like those of light, are colourless when
unbroken.
Henry W. Longfellow

Happiness grows at our own firesides, and is not to be picked in
strangers' gardens.
Douglas Jerrold

Happiness is where we find it, but rarely where we seek it.
J. Petit Senn

To be happy, we must not be too concerned with others.
Albert Camus

Happiness depends upon ourselves.
Aristotle

Try to be happy in this present moment, and put not off being so
to a time to come, as though that time should be of another make
from this which has already come and is ours.
Thomas Fuller

Knowledge of what is possible is the beginning of happiness.
George Santayana

No man is happy who does not think himself so.
Publilius Syrus

Our minds are as different as our faces: we are all traveling to one destination; --happiness; but few are going by the same road.
Charles Caleb Colton

Great quotes on Sports

Skill and confidence are an unconquered army.
George Herbert

If you aren't going all the way, why go at all?
Joe Namath

Victory belongs to the most persevering.
Napoleon Bonaparte

You are the handicap you must face.
You are the one who must choose your place.
James Lane Allen

Sports serve society by providing vivid examples of excellence.
George F. Will

There are no gains without pains.
Adlai Stevenson

If at first you don't succeed, try, try again.
William Edward Hickson

To win without risk is to triumph without glory.
Corneille

They can because they think they can.
Virgil

They wil rise highest who strive for the highest place.
(Altius ibunt qui as summa nituntur.)
Latin Proverb

Never say die.
Proverb
Most ball games are lost, not won.
Casey Stengel

It isn't hard to be good from time to time in sports.
What's tough is being good every day.
Willie Mays

You are never a loser until you quit trying.
Mike Ditka

If you can't accept losing, you can't win.
Vince Lombardi

Nothing succeeds like success.
Proverb

There is no success without hardship.
Sophocles

The virtue lies in the struggle, not the prize.
R.M. Milnes

Great quotes on Imagination

The imagination exercises a powerful influence over every act of
sense, thought, reason,
-- over every idea.
Latin Proverb

Solitude is as needful to the imagination as society is wholesome
for the character.
James Russel Lowell

Far away in the sunshine are my highest aspirations. I may not
reach them, but I can look up and see their beauty, believe in
them, and try to follow where they lead.
Louisa May Alcott

Imagination is more important than knowledge.
Albert Einstein

He who has imagination without learning, has wings and no feet.
Joseph Joubert

Hope is the dream of a man awake.
French Proverb

A strong imagination begetteth opportunity.
Michel de Montaigne

Your imagination is your preview of life's coming attractions.
Albert Einstein

Where beams of imagination play,
The memory's soft figures melt away.
Alexander Pope

Believe that you have it, and you have it.
Latin Proverb

The real voyage of discovery consists not in seeking new landscapes but in having new eyes.
Marcel Proust

The imagination is the secret and marrow of civilization.
Henry Ward Beecher

Imagine every day to be the last of a life surrounded with hopes, cares, anger, and fear. The hours that come unexpectedly will be so much more the grateful.
Horace

We don't live in a world of reality.
We live in a world of perceptions.
Gerald J. Simmons

Imagination is the eye of the soul.
Joseph Joubert

You cannot depend on your eyes when your imagination is out of focus.
Mark Twain

The human race is governed by its imagination.
Napoleon Bonaparte

Great quotes on Dreams

I have spread my dreams beneath your feet. Tread softly because you tread on my dreams.
W.B. Yeats

Go confidently in the direction of your dreams. Live the life you have imagined.
Henry David Thoreau

Every great dream begins with a dreamer. Always remember, you have within you the strength, the patience, and the passion to reach for the stars to change the world.
Harriet Tubman

Reach high, for stars lie hidden in your soul. Dream deep, for every dream precedes the goal.
Pamela Vaull Starr

All men dream but not equally. Those who dream by night in the dusty recesses of their minds wake in the day to find that it was vanity; but the dreamers of the day are dangerous men, for they may act their dream with open eyes to make it possible.
T.E. Lawrence

Our truest life is when we are in dreams awake.
Henry David Thoreau

So often times it happens that we live our lives in chains
And we never even know we have the key.
Lyrics from Already Gone, performed by the Eagles for their 1974 On the Border album

The end of wisdom is to dream high enough not to lose the dream in the seeking of it.
William Faulkner

I like the dreams of the future better than the history of the past.
Patrick Henry

Trust the dream for hidden in them is the gate to eternity.
Kahlil Gibran

Hold fast to dreams, for if dreams die, life is a broken winged
bird that cannot fly.
Lanston Hughes

You cannot dream yourself into a character: you must hammer
and forge yourself into one.
Henry D. Thoreau

The future belongs to those who believe in the beauty of their
dreams.
Eleanor Roosevelt

Commitment leads to action. Action brings your dream closer.
Marcia Wieder

Dreams are the touchstones of our character.
Henry David Thoreau

The question for each man to settle is not what he would do if he
had means, time, influence and educational advantages; the
question is what he will do with the things he has. The moment a
young man ceases to dream or to bemoan his lack of
opportunities and resolutely looks his conditions in the face, and
resolves to change them, he lays the corner-stone of a solid and
honourable success.
Hamilton Wright Mabie

The best way to make your dreams come true is to wake up.
Paul Valery

A skilful man reads his dreams for self-knowledge, yet not the details but the quality.
Ralph Waldo Emerson

Our waking hours form the text of our lives, our dreams, the commentary.
Anonymous

Hope is the dream of the waking man.
French Proverb

To unpathed waters, undreamed shores.
William Shakepeare

Great quotes on Time

Time and space are fragments of the infinite for the use of finite creatures.
Henri Frederic Amiel

Dost thou love life, then do not squander time,
for that's the stuff life is made of.
Benjamin Franklin

Time in its aging course teaches all things.
Aeschylus

Make use of time, let not advantage slip.
William Shakespeare

One cannot manage too many affairs: like pumpkins in the water, one pops up while you try to hold down the other.
Chinese Proverb

You will never "find" time for anything. If you want time, you must make it.
Charles Bruxton

I recommend you take care of the minutes and the hours will take care of themselves.
Earl of Chesterfield

To do two things at once is to do neither.
Publius Syrus

A man who dares waste one hour of time has not discovered the value of life.
Charles Darwin

The laws of science do not distinguish between the past and the future.
Steven W. Hawking

Time and tide wait for no man.
Geoffrey Chaucer

I have yet to hear a man ask for advice on how to combine
marriage and a career.
Gloria Steinem from
Work at Home Moms
Time Management Tips

Time is a file that wears and makes no noise.
English Proverb

He lives long that lives well; and time misspent is not lived but
lost.
Thomas Fuller

Take time: much may be gained by patience.
Latin Proverb

Take care of the minutes and the hours will take care of
themselves.
Lord Chesterfield

There is time for everything.
Thomas A. Edison

Spare moments are the gold dust of time.
Bishop Hail

The swiftness of time is infinite, as is still more evident when we
look back on the past.
Seneca

Time is but the shadow of the world upon the background of
eternity.
Jerome K. Jerome

Thrift of time will repay you in after-life with a thousand fold of profit beyond your most sanguine dreams.
William E. Gladstone

You may as well borrow a person's money as his time.
Horace Mann

You will never find time for anything. If you want time you must make it.
Charles Buxton

Those that make the best use of their time have none to spare.
Thomas Fuller

To comprehend a man's life, it is necessary to know not merely what he does but also what he purposely leaves undone. There is a limit to the work that can be got out of a human body or a human brain, and he is a wise man who wastes no energy on pursuits for which he is not fitted; and he is till wiser who, from among the things that he can do well, chooses and resolutely follows the best.
John Hall Gladstone

Time, which changes people, does not alter the image we have of them.
Marcel Proust

Time is a physician which heals every grief.
Diphilus

Gaining time is gaining everything in love, trade and war.
John Shebbeare

Time is money.
Benjamin Franklin

You cannot step twice into the same river, for other waters are continually flowing on.
Heraclitus

The more business a man has to do, the more he is able to accomplish, for he learns to economize his time.
Sir Matthew Hale

The worst thing you can try to do is cling to something that is gone, or to recreate it.
Johnette Napolitano

Time is but the stream I go fishing in.
Henry David Thoreau

He who know most grieves most for wasted time.
Dante

You can ask me for anything you like, except time.
Napoleon Bonaparte

Great quotes on Leadership

Do not follow where the path may lead.
Go instead where there is no path and leave a trail.
Harold R. McAlindon
(also attributed to Emerson and others)

Leadership: The art of getting someone else to do something you
want done because he wants to do it.
Dwight D. Eisenhower

There go the people.
I must follow them for I am their leader.
Alexandre Ledru-Rollin

What chance gathers she easily scatters. A great person attracts
great people and knows how to hold them together.
Johann Wolfgang Von Goethe

A general is just as good or just as bad as the troops under his
command make him.
General Douglas MacArthur

Men are governed only by serving them; the rule is without
exception.
V. Cousin

The real leader has no need to lead--
he is content to point the way.
Henry Miller

Not the cry, but the flight of a wild duck, leads the flock to fly and
follow.
Chinese Proverb

Be known for pleasing others, especially if you govern them...Ruling other has one advantage: you can do more good than anyone else.
Baltasar Gracián

Go to the people. Learn from them. Live with them. Start with what they know. Build with what they have. The best of leaders when the job is done, when the task is accomplished, the people will say we have done it ourselves.
Lao Tzu

A leader is a dealer in hope.
Napoleon Bonaparte

Rely on your own strength of body and soul. Take for your star self-reliance, faith, honesty and industry. Don't take too much advice — keep at the helm and steer your own ship, and remember that the great art of commanding is to take a fair share of the work. Fire above the mark you intend to hit. Energy, invincible determination with the right motive, are the levers that move the world.
Noah Porter

He that would be a leader must also be a bridge.
Welsh Proverb

There is always room for a man of force and he makes room for many. Society is a troop of thinkers and the best heads among them take the best places.
Ralph Waldo Emerson

If your actions inspire others to dream more, learn more, do more and become more, you are a leader.
John Quincy Adams

He who has never learned to obey
cannot be a good commander.
Aristotle

The ultimate measure of a man is not where he stands in moments of comfort, but where he stands at times of challenge and controversy.
Martin Luther King, Jr.
(from Christian Leadership World)

Any one can hold the helm when the sea is calm.
Publilius Syrus

A leader is a dealer in hope.
Napoleon Bonaparte

Never tell people how to do things. Tell them what to do and they will surprise you with their ingenuity.
George Patton
(from Big Dog's Quotes)

Where there is no vision, the people perish.
Proverbs 29:18

Misfortunes, untoward events, lay open, disclose the skill of a general, while success conceals his weakness, his weak points.
Horace

In this world a man must either be an anvil or hammer.
Henry W. Longfellow

I light my candle from their torches.
Robert Burton

Leadership does not always wear the harness of compromise.
Woodrow Wilson

The greater a man is in power above others, the more he ought to excel them in virtue. None ought to govern who is not better than the governed.
Publius Syrus

A bold onset is half the battle.
Giuseppe Garibaldi

The power is detested, and miserable the life, of him who wishes
to be feared rather than to be loved.
Cornelius Nepos

To be a great leader and so always master of the situation, one
must of necessity have been a great thinker in action. An eagle
was never yet hatched from a goose's egg.
James Thomas

Ill can he rule the great that cannot reach the small.
Edmund Spenser

He who has learned how to obey will know how to command.
Solon

When I give a minister an order, I leave it to him to find the
means to carry it out.
Napoleon Bonaparte

No man can stand on top because he is put there.
H. H. Vreeland

A ruler should be slow to punish and swift to reward.
Ovid

It is impossible to imagine anything, which better becomes a
ruler than mercy.
Seneca

No man is good enough to govern another man without that
other's consent.
Abraham Lincoln

What you cannot enforce /
Do not command.
Sophocles

No general can fight his battles alone. He must depend upon his
lieutenants, and his success depends upon his ability to select
the right man for the right place.
Philip Armour

To do great things is difficult; but to command great things is
more difficult.
Friedrich Nietzsche

It is absurd that a man should rule others, who cannot rule
himself.
(*Absurdum est ut alios regat, qui seipsum regere nescit.*)
Latin Proverb

Let him who would be moved to convince others, be first moved
to convince himself.
Thomas Carlyle

The measure of a man is what he does with power.
Greek Proverb

A good general not only sees the way to victory; he also knows
when victory is impossible.
Polybius

Great quotes on Literature and Libraries

The only true equalisers in the world are books; the only treasure-house open to all comers is a library; the only wealth which will not decay is knowledge; the only jewel which you can carry beyond the grave is wisdom.
J. A. Langford

It is, however, not to the museum, or the lecture-room, or the drawing-school, but to the library, that we must go for the completion of our humanity. It is books that bear from age to age the intellectual wealth of the world.
Owen Meredith

In the houses of the humble a little library in my opinion is a most precious possession.
John Bright

A blessed companion is a book!
A book that is fitly chosen is a life-long friend.
Douglas Jerrod

No possession can surpass, or even equal, a good library to the lover of books.
J. A. Langford

Me, poor man, my library
Was dukedom large enough.
William Shakespeare, The Tempest

A little library, growing larger every year, is an honourable part of a man's history. It is a man's duty to have books. A library is not a luxury, but one of the necessaries of life.
Henry Ward Beecher

The library of a good man is one of his most constant, cheerful, and instructive companions; and as it has delighted him in youth, so will it solace him in old age.
C. Frognall Dibdin

How still and peaceful is a Library! It seems quiet as the grave, tranquil as heaven, a cool collection of the thoughts of the men of all times. And yet, approach and open the pages, and you find them full of dissension and disputes, alive with abuse and detraction— a huge, many-volumed satire upon man, written by himself. . . . What a broad thing is a library — all shades of opinion reflected on its catholic bosom, as the sunbeams and shadows of a summer's day upon the ample mirror of a lake.
George Gilfillan

Every man should have a library....And when we have got our little library we may look proudly at Shakespeare, and Bacon, and Bunyan, as they stand in our bookcase in company with other noble spirits, and one or two of whom the world knows nothing, but whose worth we have often tested. These may cheer and enlighten us, may inspire us with higher aims and aspirations, may make us, if we use them rightly, wiser and better men.
William A. E. Axon

What a place to be in is an old library! It seems as though all the souls of all the writers that have bequeathed their labours to these Bodleians, were reposing here as in some dormitory, or middle state.
Charles Lamb

Knowledge is of two kinds. We know a subject ourselves, or we know where we can find information upon it. When we enquire into any subject, the first thing we have to do, is to know what books have treated of it. This leads us to look at catalogues, and the backs of books in libraries.
Samuel Johnson

A scholar must shape his own shell; secrete it, one might almost say, for secretion is only separation, you know, of certain elements derived from the materials of the world about us. And a scholar's study, with the books lining its walls, is his shell.
Oliver Wendell Holmes

In my garden I spend my days; in my library I spend my nights. My interests are divided between my geraniums and my books. With the flower I am in the present; with the book I am in the past. I go into my library, and all history unrolls before me.
Alexander Smith

The truest owner of a Library is he who has bought each book for the love he bears to it; who is happy and content to say,—" Here are my jewels; my choicest material possessions.
Frank Carr

A very short examination of a library is sufficient to enable one to describe the owner in general and unmistakable terms.
Author Unkown

Life transforming ideas have always come to me through books.
Oliver Wendall Holmes

A book without an index is like a compass without a needle.
Anonymous

Any kid who has two parents who are interested in him and a houseful of books isn't poor.
Sam Levenson

Books cannot always please, however good;
Minds are not ever craving for their food.
George Crabbe

In books lies the soul of the whole past time.
Thomas Carlyle

We find little in books but what we put there.
But in great books, the mind finds room to put many things.
Joseph Joubert

Books are the windows through which the soul looks out.
Henry Ward Beecher

Read the best books first,
or you may not have a chance to read them all.
Henry David Thoreau

Do give books - religious or otherwise - for Christmas. They're
never fattening, seldom sinful, and permanently personal.
Lenore Hershey

People will not be better than the books they read.
Bishop Potter

A good book is the precious life-blood
of a master spirit, embalmed and treasured
up on purpose to a life beyond life.
John Milton

For a good book is the best of friends, the same to-day and for
ever.
Martin Farqubar Tupper

Books are not made for furniture, but there is nothing else that
so beautifully furnishes a house.
Henry Ward Beecher

"Classic": A book which people praise but don't read.
Mark Twain

You can't tell a book by its movie.
Louis A Safian

A book may be compared to your neighbour:
if it be good it cannot last too long;
if bad, you cannot get rid of it too early.
Henry Brooke

Great quotes on Writing

Talent alone cannot make a writer.
There must be a man behind the book.
Ralph Waldo Emerson

One man is as good as another until he has written a book.
Benjamin Jowett

Think much, speak little, and write less.
Italian Proverb

The secret of all good writing is sound judgment.
Horace

The ink of the scholar is more sacred than the blood of the martyr.
Mohammed

To write well is to think well, to feel well, and to render well; it is to possess at once intellect, soul, and taste.
George-Louis Leclerc de Buffon

Superlatives are diminutives, and weaken.
Ralph Waldo Emerson

A man will turn over half a library to make one book.
Samuel Johnson

What a joy is there in a good book, writ by some great master of thought, who breaks into beauty, as in summer the meadow into grass and dandelions and violets.
Theodore Parker

It makes little difference how many university degrees or courses a person may own. If he cannot use words to move an idea from one point to another, his education is incomplete.
Norman Cousins

But words are things, and a small drop of ink,
Falling like dew upon a thought, produces
That which makes thousands, perhaps millions, think.
Lord Byron

In good writing, words become one with things.
Ralph Waldo Emerson

Once the itch of literature comes over a man, nothing can scratch
it but a pen.
Samuel Lover

If you wish to be a writer, write.
Epictetus

To write without clarity or charm is a miserable waste of time
and ink.
Cicero

A collection of good sentences resembles a string of pearls.
Chinese Proverb

Beneath the rule of men entirely great,
The pen is mightier than the sword.
Edward Bulwer Lytton

Successful writers learn at last what they should learn at first,--
to be intelligently simple.
Josh Billings

If a book comes from the heart, it will contrive to reach other
hearts; all art and author craft are of small amount to that.
Thomas Carlyle

Proper words in proper places make the true definition of a
style.
Jonathan Swift

Whatever sentence will bear to be read twice, we may be sure was thought twice.
Henry David Thoreau

You don't write because you want to say something;
you write because you've got something to say.
F. Scott Fitzgerald

We never know how much has been missing from our lives until a true writer comes along.
Alfred Kazin

Reading maketh a full man, conference a ready man, and writing an exact man.
Lord Bacon

Great quotes on Reading

People say life is the thing, but I prefer reading.
Logan Pearsall Smith

Books worth reading are worth re-reading.
Holbrook Jackson

What refuge is there for the victim who is oppressed with the
feeling that there are a thousand new books he ought to read,
while life is only long enough for him to attempt a hundred?
Oliver Wendall Holmes, Sr.

To read a writer is for me not merely to get an
idea of what he says, but to go off with him,
and travel in his company.
Andre Gride

Reading furnishes the mind only with the materials of
knowledge; it is thinking that makes what we read ours.
John Locke

Let us read good works often over. Some skip from volume to
volume, touching on all points, resting on none. We hold, on the
contrary, that, if a book be worth reading once, it is worth
reading twice, and that if it stands a second reading, it may stand
a third.
George Gilfillan

I have lost all sense of home, having moved about so much. It
means to me now - only that place where the books are kept.
John Steinbeck

Books are the treasured wealth of the world
and the fit inheritance of generations and nations.
Henry David Thoreau

A fondness for reading changes the inevitable dull hours of our
life into exquisite hours of delight.
Charles de Montesquieu

I would rather be a poor man in a garret with plenty of books
than a king who did not love reading.
Thomas B. Macaulay

Books worth reading are worth reading twice;
and what is most important of all, the masterpieces of literature
are worth reading a thousand times.
John Morley

I love to lose myself in other men's mind's.
When I am not walking, I am reading;
I cannot sit and think. Books think for me.
Georg Christoph Lichtenberg

Great quotes on Goals

The ability to convert ideas to things is the secret to outward
success.
Henry Ward Beecher

The ability to concentrate and to use your time well is everything
if you want to succeed in business--or almost anywhere else for
that matter.
Lee Iacocca

A wise man will make more opportunities than he finds.
Francis Bacon

In everything the ends well defined are the secret of durable
success.
Victor Cousins

Winning isn't everything, but wanting to win is.
Vince Lombardi

Failures do what is tension relieving,
while winners do what is goal achieving.
Dennis Waitley
(as quoted in Brian Tracy's book, Eat That Frog)

A man should have any number of little aims about which he
should be conscious and for which he should have names, but he
should have neither name for, nor consciousness concerning, the
main aim of his life.
Samuel Butler

Goals are the fuel in the furnace of achievement.
Brian Tracy, Eat that Frog

The great and glorious masterpiece of
man is to know how to live to purpose.
Michel de Montaigne

Ah, but a man's reach should exceed his grasp,
or what's a heaven for?
Robert Browning

The significance of a man is not in what he attains but in what he
longs to attain.
Kahlil Gibran

Every ceiling, when reached, becomes a floor, upon which one
walks as a matter of course and prescriptive right.
Aldous Huxley

If you don't know where you are going,
you'll end up someplace else.
Yogi Berra

Some men give up their designs when they have almost reached
the goal; while others; on the contrary, obtain a victory by
exerting, at the last moment, more vigorous efforts than before.
Polybius

Life can be pulled by goals just as surely as it can be pushed by
drives.
Viktor Frankl

The virtue lies in the struggle, not in the prize.
Richard Monckton Milnes

To reach a port, we must sail—Sail, not tie at anchor—Sail, not
drift.
Franklin Roosevelt

There is no happiness except in the realization that we have
accomplished something.
Henry Ford

Our plans miscarry because they have no aim. When a man does not know what harbour he is making for, no wind is the right wind.
Seneca

It is not enough to take steps, which may some day lead to a goal; each step must be itself a goal and a step likewise.
Johann Wolfgang von Goethe

Who aims at excellence will be above mediocrity; who aims at mediocrity will be far short of it.
Burmese Saying

In absence of clearly defined goals, we become strangely loyal to performing daily acts of trivia.
Author Unknown

It is better to fall short of a high mark than to reach a low one.
H. C. Payne

Don't bunt. Aim out of the ballpark.
David Ogilvy

There are two things to aim at in life; first to get what you want, and after that to enjoy it. Only the wisest of mankind has achieved the second.
Logan Pearsall Smith

Great quotes on Education

Education make a people easy to lead, but difficult to drive: easy
to govern, but impossible to enslave.
Peter Brougham

Education is not the filling of a pail,
but the lighting of a fire.
Wiliam Butler Yeats

Tell me and I'll forget. Show me, and I may not remember.
Involve me, and I'll understand.
Native American Saying

What we learn with pleasure we never forget.
Alfred Mercier

Education is simply the soul of a society as it passes from one
generation to another.
G. K. Chesterson

Instruction ends in the schoolroom, but education ends only
with life.
Frederick W.Robertson

It is in fact a part of the function of education to help us escape,
not from our own time -- for we are bound by that -- but from
the intellectual and emotional limitations of our time.
T.S. Eliot

Whatever is good to know is difficult to learn.
Greek Proverb

What sculpture is to a block of marble,
education is to the human soul.
Joseph Addison

What we have learned from other becomes our own reflection.
Ralph Waldo Emerson

If a nation expects to be ignorant and free, in a state of
civilization, it expects what never was and will never be.
Thomas Jefferson

Practice is the best of all instructors.
Publilius Syrus

Education is the transmission of civilization.
Will Durant

It is a greater work to educate a child, in the true and larger
sense of the word, than to rule a state.
William Ellery Channing

Education is more than a luxury; it is a responsibility that society
owes to itself.
Robin Cook

Let us never be betrayed into saying we have finished our
education; because that would mean we had stopped growing.
Julia H. Gulliver

Character is a wish for a perfect education.
Novalis

The fruit of liberal education is not learning, but the capacity and
desire to learn, not knowledge, but power.
Charles W. Eliot

The ultimate goal of the educational system is to shift to the
individual the burden of pursuing his education.
John W. Gardner

Intelligence plus character--that is the goal of true education.
Martin Luther King, Jr.

I am still learning.
Michelangelo

Next in importance to freedom and justice is popular education,
without which which neither freedom nor justice can be
maintained.
James A. Garfield

Education, like the mass of our age's inventions, is after all, only
a tool; everything depends upon the workman who uses it
The Simple Life

Learning is like rowing upstream:
not to advance is to drop back.
Chinese Saying

Education should bring to light the ideal of the individual.
J.P Richter

Education should consist of a series of enchantments, each
raising the individual to a higher level of awareness,
understanding, and kinship with all living things.
Author Unknown

When asked how much educated men were superior to those
uneducated, Aristotle answered, 'As much as the living are to the
dead.'
Diogenes Laetius

Upon the education of the people of this country, the fate of this
country depends.
Benjamin Disraeli

Education is the best provision for old age.
Aristotle

Great quotes on Teaching

A teacher affects eternity:
he can never tell where his influence stops.
Henry Adams

What nobler employment, or more valuable to the state, than
that of the man who instructs the rising generation.
Marcus Tullius Cicero

The important thing is not so much
that every child should be taught,
as that every child should be given the wish to learn.
John Lubbock

Those who educate children well are more to be honored than
parents, for these only gave life,
those the art of living well.
Aristotle

What office is there which involves more responsibility, which
requires more qualifications, and which ought, therefore, to be
more honorable than teaching?
Harriet Martineau

By learning you will teach;
by teaching you will understand.
Latin Proverb

Education is the mother of leadership.
Wendell L. Willkie

Seldom was any knowledge given to keep, but to impart; the
grace of this rich jewel is lost in concealment.
Bishop Hall

If you would thoroughly know anything, teach it to others.
Tryon Edwards

We cannot hold a torch to light another's path without
brightening our own.
Ben Sweetland

Grammar speaks; dialectics teach us truth; rhetoric gives
colouring to our speech; music sings; arithmetic numbers;
geometry weighs and measures;
astronomy teaches us to know the stars.
Latin Maxim

To know how to suggest is the great art of teaching.
Henri Frederic Amiel

We learn by teaching.
James Howell

Natural ability is by far the best, but many men have succeeded
in winning high renown by skill that is the fruit of teaching.
Pindar

It is the supreme art of the teacher to awaken
joy in creative expression and knowledge.
Albert Einstein

The most effective teacher will always be biased,
for the chief force in teaching is confidence and enthusiasm.
Joyce Cary

Education is the guardian genius of democracy.
It is the only dictator that free men recognize,
and the only ruler that free men require.
Mirabeau Buonaparte Lamar

Whatever you want to teach, be brief.
Horace

To me, education is a leading out of what is already there in the pupil's soul.
Muriel Spark

Nine-tenths of education is encouragement.
Anatole France

The true aim of every one who aspires to be a teacher should be,
not to impart his own opinions,
but to kindle minds.
F. W. Robertson

He that teaches us anything which we knew not
before is undoubtedly to be reverenced as a master.
Samuel Johnson

I hear and I forget. I see and I remember.
I do and I understand.
Chinese Proverb
From Teaching Quotations at Parrot's Meow

Be careful to leave your sons well
instructed rather than rich,
for the hopes of the instructed are better
than the wealth of the ignorant.
Epictetus

I am indebted to my father for living, but to my teacher for living well.
Alexander of Macedon

To know how to suggest is the great art of teaching. To attain it we must be able to guess what will interest: we must learn to read the childish soul as we might a piece of music. Then, by simply changing the key, we keep up the attraction anil vary the song.
Henri Frederic Amiel

Teaching is not a lost art,
but the regard for it is a lost tradition.
Jacques Barzun

Education is the transmission of civilization.
Will Durant

To teach is to learn twice over.
Joseph Joubert

A schoolmaster should have an atmosphere of awe,
and walk wonderingly, as if he was amazed at being himself.
Newton D. Baker

One good teacher in a lifetime may sometimes
change a delinquent into a solid citizen.
Philip Wylie

A child mis-educated is a child lost.
John F. Kennedy

A master can tell you what he expects of you.
A teacher, though, awakens your own expectations.
Patricia Neal

Never try to teach a pig to sing.
It wastes your time and annoys the pig.
Anonymous

Great quotes on Self-Improvement

Employ your time in improving yourself by other men's writings so that you shall come easily by what others have labored hard for.
Socrates

People seldom improve when they have no other model but themselves to copy.
Oliver Goldsmith

Let us strive to improve ourselves, for we cannot remain stationary; one either progresses or retrogrades.
Mme. du Deffand

The safest principle through life, instead of reforming others, is to set about perfecting yourself.
B. R. Haydon

Change yourself and fortune will change with you.
Portugese Proverb

What you dislike in another take care to correct in yourself.
Thomas Sprat

The highest purpose of intellectual cultivation is to give a man a perfect knowledge and mastery of his own inner self; to render our consciousness its own light and its own mirror.
Frederich Leopold von Hardenberg

In this world man must either be anvil or hammer.
Henry W. Longfellow

What are the aims which are at the same time duties? They are perfecting of ourselves, the happiness of others.
Immanuel Kant

Many only learns in two ways, one by reading, and the other by association with smarter people.
Will Rogers

Every man has in himself a continent of undiscovered character. Happy is he who acts as the Columbus to his own soul.
Sir J. Stephen

Too low they build, who build beneath the stars.
Edward Young

Discontent is the source of all trouble,
but also of all progress, in individuals and nations.
Berthold Auerbach

Slumber not in the tents of your fathers! The world is advancing. Advance with it!
Mazzini

The greatest of faults, I should say, is to be conscious of none.
Thomas Carlyle

Hold yourself responsible for a higher standard than anyone else expects of you.
Never excuse yourself.
Henry Ward Beecher

It was the sacred rule among the Pythagoreans that they should every evening thrice run over the actions and affairs of the day.
Dr. L. Watts

Never neglect an opportunity for improvement.
Sir William Jones

Remedy your deficiencies,
and your merits will take care of themselves.
Edward Bulwer-Lytton

Look within, for within is the wellspring of virtue, which will not cease flowing, if you cease not from digging.
Marcus Aurelius

Everyone has naturally the power of excelling in some one thing.
Proverb

The Athenians, alarmed at the internal decay of their Republic, asked Demosthenes what to do.
His reply: "Do not do what you are doing now."
Joseph Ray

Circumspection in calamity; mercy in greatness; good speeches in assemblies; fortitude in adversity: these are the self-attained perfections of great souls.
Hitopadesa

Practice yourself in little things, and thence proceed to greater.
Epictetus

If you have great talents, industry will improve them; If moderate abilities, industry will supply their deficiencies. Nothing is denied to well-directed labour: nothing is ever to be attained without it.
Sir Joshua Reynolds

There is nothing noble about being superior to some other man. The true nobility is in being superior to your previous self.
Hindu Proverb

What you are must always displease you, if you would attain to that which you are not.
Saint Augustine

Live up to the best that is in you: Live noble lives, as you all may, in whatever condition you may find yourselves.
Henry W. Longfellow

Great quotes on Teamwork

Divide the fire and you will soon put it out.
Greek Proverb

All for one and one for all.
Motto from the Three Musketeeers, by Alexandre Dumas

Many hands make light work.
English Proverb

Three, helping one another, bear the burden of six.
Latin Proverb

When spider webs unite, they can tie up a lion.
Ethiopian Proverb

No man is an island.
John Donne

By appreciation, we make excellence in others our own property.
Voltaire

When was ever honey made with one bee in a hive?
Thomas Hood

United we stand, divided we fall.
Aesop

He who cannot help many hinders.
German Proverb

A willing helper does not wait until he is asked.
Danish Proverb

One right and honest definition of business is mutual
helpfulness.
William Feather

Unity is a precious diamond.
Holyday

Light is the task where many share the toil.
Homer

It is good to rub and polish our brains against that of others.
Michel de Montaigne

If I have seen further it is by standing on the shoulders of giants.
Isaac Newton

A chain is only as stong as its weakest link.
Scottish Proverb

Great quotes on Achievement

No one can possibly achieve any real and lasting success or "get rich" in business by being a conformist.
J. Paul Getty

No road is too long for him who advances slowly and does not hurry, and no attainment is beyond his reach that equips himself with patience to achieve it.
Jean de La Bruyère

Thomas Edison dreamed of a lamp that could be operated by electricity, began where he stood to put his dream into action, and despite more than ten thousand failures, he stood by that dream until he made it a physical reality.
Practical dreamers do not quit.
Napoleon Hill

Those who believe they are exclusively in the right are generally those who achieve something.
Aldous Huxley

Dreams seldom materialise on their own.
Dian Fossey

Genius begins great works; labour alone finishes them.
Joseph Joubert

Vigilance in watching opportunity; tact and daring in seizing upon opportunity; force and persistence in crowding opportunity to its utmost of possible achievement — these are the martial virtues which must command success.
Austin Phelps

Whatsoever the mind has ordained for itself, it has achieved.
Seneca

I attempt an arduous task; but there is no worth in that which is not a difficult achievement.
Ovid

The shortest way to do many things is to do only one thing at a time.
Richard Cech

Effort only fully releases its reward after a person refuses to quit.
Napoleon Hill

The secret of all great undertakings is hard work and self-reliance.
Gustavus F. Swift

Shallow men believe in luck, strong men believe in cause and effect.
Ralph Waldo Emerson

People sometimes attribute my success to my genius; all the genius I know anything about is hard work.
Alexander Hamilton

Success is sweet, the sweeter if long delayed and attained through maul fold struggles and defeats.
A. Bronson Alcott

Much we learn only to forget it again; to stand by the goal, we must traverse all the way to it.
Rückert

Not the maker of plans and promises, but rather the one who offers faithful service in small matters. This is the person who is most likely to achieve what is good and lasting.
Johann Wolfgang von Goethe

Great men are the modellers, patterns, and in wider sense creators, of whatsoever the general mass of men contrived to do and attain.
Carlyle

If the mass of people hesitate to act, strike thou in swift with all boldness; the noble heart that understands and seizes quick hold of opportunity can achieve everything.
Johann Wolfgang von Goethe

I will either find the way – or make one
(*Aut viam inveniam, aut faciam*)
Hannibal

Great quotes on Overcoming Adversity

There is no education like adversity.
Benjamin Disraeli

In prosperity, our friends know us; in adversity, we know our friends.
John Churton Collins

Nothing is predestined: The obstacles of your past can become the gateways that lead to new beginnings.
Ralph Blum

Difficulties strengthen the mind, as well as labour does the body.
Seneca

Without sweat and toil no work is made perfect.
Latin Proverb

It has been my philosophy of life that difficulties vanish when faced boldly.
Isaac Asimov

Good fortune and bad are equally necessary to man, to fit him to meet the contingencies of this life.
French Proverb

It is interesting to notice how some minds seem almost to create themselves, springing up under every disadvantage, and working their solitary but irresistible way through a thousand obstacles.
Washington Irving

You may find the worst enemy or best friend in yourself.
English Proverb

Heaven never helps the man who will not act.
Sophocles

Every noble work is at first impossible.
Thomas Carlyle

Adversity is the diamond dust heaven polishes its jewels with.
Robert Leighton

The man of virtue makes the difficulty to be overcome his first
business, and success only a subsequent consideration.
Confucius

All misfortune is but a stepping-stone to fortune.
Henry David Thoreau

Fractures well cured make us stronger.
Ralph Waldo Emerson

Adversity is wont to reveal genius, prosperity to hide it.
Horace

Misfortunes often sharpen the genius.
Ovid

The rays of happiness, like those of light, are colourless when
unbroken.
Henry W. Longfellow

Success in the affairs of life often serves to hide one's abilities,
whereas adversity frequently gives one an opportunity to
discover them.
Horace

Look not mournfully into the past, it comes not back again.
Wisely improve the present, it is thine. Go forth to meet the
shadowy future without fear and with a manly heart.
Henry Wadsworth Longfellow

A gentleman can withstand hardships; it is only the small man who, when submitted to them, is swept off his feet.
Confucius

Little minds are tamed and subdued by misfortune, but great minds rise above them.
Washington Irving

Difficulties strengthen the mind,
as well as labour does the body.
Seneca

Times of great calamity and confusion have ever been productive of the greatest minds. The purest ore is produced from the hottest furnace, and the brightest thunderbolt is elicited from the darkest storm.
Charles Caleb Colton

The gem cannot be polished without friction, nor man be perfected without trials.
Danish Proverb

Obstacles are great incentives.
Jules Michelet

There is no excellence uncoupled with difficulties.
Ovid

The art of living lies less in eliminating our troubles than in growing with them.
Bernard M. Baruch

In the midst of winter, I found there was within me an invincible summer.
Albert Careb

Surmounted difficulties not only teach, but hearten us in our
future struggles.
James Sharp

A wise man adapts himself to circumstances as water shapes
itself to the vessel that contains it.
Chinese Proverb

Problems are only opportunities in work clothes.
Henry J. Kaiser

Look up and not down; look forward and not back; look out and
not in; and lend a hand.
E. E. Hale

What is defeat?
Nothing but the first steps to something better.
Proverb

Sweet are the uses of adversity,
Which like the toad, ugly and venomous,
Wears yet a precious jewel in his head.
William Shakespeare

It is the surmounting of difficulties that make heroes.
Louis Kossuth

Wherever we look upon this earth, the opportunities take shape
within the problems.
Nelson A. Rockefeller

Prosperity is a great teacher; adversity a greater.
William Hazlitt

Difficulties, by bracing the mind to overcome them, assist
cheerfulness, as exercise assists digestion.
Christian Nestell Bovee

A wretched soul, bruis'd with adversity,
We bid be quiet, when we hear it cry;
But were we burthen'd with like weight of pain,
As much, or more, we should ourselves complain.
William Shakespeare

In adversity those talents are called forth which are concealed by prosperity. Horace

It will not always be summer.
(*non semper erit aestas*)
Erasmus

Great quotes on Perseverance

Our greatest glory consists not in never falling, but in rising every time we fall.
Oliver Goldsmith

The block of granite which was an obstacle in the pathway of the weak, became a stepping-stone in the pathway of the strong.
Thomas Carlyle

Press on! A better fate awaits thee.
Victor Hugo

Perseverance is king.
Josh Billings

The waters wear the stones.
The Book of Job 14:19

Energy and persistence conquer all things.
Benjamin Franklin

Our greatest glory is not in never falling but in rising every time we fall.
Confucius

The man who removes a mountain begins by carrying away small stones.
Chinese Proverb

I demolish my bridges behind me. Then there is no choice but to move forward.
Firdtjof Nansen

Nothing great is created suddenly, any more than a bunch of grapes or a fig.
Epictetus

The important thing in life is to have great aim and to possess the aptitude and the perseverance to attain it.
Johann Wolfgang Von Goethe

Success in life is a matter not so much of talent or opportunity as of concentration and perseverance.
C. W. Wendte

I hold a doctrine, to which I owe not much, indeed, but all the little I ever had, namely, that with ordinary talent and extraordinary perseverance, all things are attainable.
Sir T. F. Buxton

Those who would attain to any marked degree of excellence in a chosen pursuit must work, and work hard for it, prince or peasant.
Bayard Taylor

It is interesting to notice how some minds seem almost to create themselves, springing up under every disadvantage, and working their solitary but irresistible way through a thousand obstacles.
Washington Irving

Let me tell you the secret that has led me to my goal. My strength lies solely in my tenacity.
Louis Pasteur

Persistent people begin their success where others end in failure.
Edward Eggleston

The drops of rain make a hole in the stone, not by violence, but by oft falling.
Lucretius 95 BC - From Perseverance:
(persistence...endurance...persevere...)
Happy Otter

He who would do some great thing in this short life, must apply himself to the work with such a concentration of his forces as to the idle spectators, who live only to amuse themselves, looks like insanity.
John Foster

Great works are performed not by strength, but by perseverance.
Samuel Johnson

Do not think that what is hard for thee to master is impossible for man; but if a thing is possible and proper to man, deem it attainable by thee.
Marcus Aurelius

It does not matter how slowly you go so long as you do not stop.
Confucius

Learn to persevere!
(*Disce pati!*)
Flavinius

Victory belongs to the most persevering.
Napoleon I

Great quotes on Communication

Be silent, or say something better than silence.
Pythagoras

Proper words in proper places make the true definition of a
style.
Jonathan Swift

It is as easy to draw back a stone, thrown with force from the
hand, as to recall a word once spoken.
Menander

Never say more than is necessary.
Richard Brinsley Sheridan

Much tongue and much judgment seldom go together.
Roger L'Estrange

If the truth were self evident, eloquence would be unnecessary.
Cicero

We never listen when we are eager to speak.
François de La Rochefoucauld

He that converses not, knows nothing.
English Proverb

It is good to rub and polish our brain
against that of others.
Montaigne

My words fly up, my thoughts remain below: Words without
thoughts, never to heaven go.
William Shakespeare, Hamlet. Act III. Sc. 3

Kind words are the music of the world.
F. W. Faber

People who have nothing to say are never at a loss in talking.
Josh Bilings

Deliver your words not by number but by weight.
Proverb

I saw one excellency that was within my reach —it was brevity;
and I determined to obtain it.
William Jay

The great thing is to know when to speak and when to keep
quiet.
Seneca the Younger

Silence is often advantageous.
Menander

Eloquence is the power to translate a truth into language
perfectly intelligible to the person to whom you speak.
Ralph Waldo Emerson

Many can argue - not many converse.
A. Bronson Alcott

The less people speak of their greatness, the more we think of it.
Sir Francis Bacon

Language is the close-fitting dress of Thought.
R. C. Trench

Good, the more communicated, more abundant grows.
John Milton

The first ingredient in conversation is truth:
the next good sense; the third, good humour;
and the fourth wit.
Sir William Temple

Be slow of tongue and quick of eye.
Cervantes

True eloquence, indeed, does not consist in speech. It cannot be brought from far. Labour and learning may toil for it, but they will toil in vain. Words and phrases may be marshalled in every way, but they cannot compass it. It must exist in the man, in the subject, and in the occasion.
Daniel Webster

Great quotes on dealing with people

You must look into other people as well as at them.
Lord Chesterfield

A good deed is never lost: he who sows courtesy reaps
friendship; and he who plants kindness gathers love.
Basil

A man's own good breeding is the best security against other
people's ill manners.
Lord Chesterfield

The secret of many a man's success in the world resides in his
insight into the moods of men and his tact in dealing with them.
J. G. Holland

To rejoice in another's prosperity, is to give content to your own
lot: to mitigate another's grief, is to alleviate or dispel your own.
Thomas Edwards

Hear the meaning within the word.
William Shakespeare

Charity, good behaviour, amiable speech, and unselfishness —
these by the chief sage have been declared the elements of
popularity.
Burmese Proverb

Kind words are the music of the world.
F. W. Faber

We are far more liable to catch the vices than the virtues of our
associates.
Denis Diderot

Arguing with a fool proves there are two.
Doris M. Smith

Be courteous to all, but intimate with few;
and let those be well-tried before you give them your confidence.
George Washington

Look to be treated by others
as you have treated others.
Publius Syrus

Success in life, in anything,
depends upon the number of persons
that one can make himself agreeable to.
Thomas Carlyle

Never part without loving words to think of during your
absence. It may be that you will not meet again in this life.
Jean Paul Richter

Let us believe neither half of the good people tell us of ourselves,
nor half of the evil they say of others.
J. Petit Senn

The more you say, the less people remember.
François Fénelon

Never lose a chance of saying a kind word.
William Thackeray

The soul of conversation is sympathy.
Thomas Campbell

It is always good to know, if only in passing, charming human
beings. It refreshes one like flowers and woods and clear brooks.
George Eliot

Every man is a volume if you know how to read him.
William Ellery Channing

Learn to regard the souls around you as parts of some grand instrument. It is for each of us to know the keys and stops, that we may draw forth the harmonies that He sleeping in the silent octaves.
Anonymous

If evil be said of thee, and if it be true, correct thyself; if it be a lie, laugh at it.
Epictetus

In many things it is not well to say, "Know thyself"; it is better to say, "Know others."
Menander

The less people speak of their greatness,
the more we think of it.
Lord Bacon

He who sedulously attends, pointedly asks, calmly speaks, coolly answers and ceases when he has no more to say is in possession of some of the best requisites of man.
Johann Casper Lavater

Men are more mindful of wrongs than of benefits.
Proverb

A good word is an easy obligation; but not to speak ill requires only our silence; which costs us nothing.
John Tillotson

It requires less character to discover the faults of others than is does to tolerate them.
J. Petit Senn

Do not forget small kindnesses and do not remember small faults.
Chinese Proverb

Great quotes on Opportunity

Great opportunities come to all but many do not know they have met them. The only preparation to take advantage of them is simple fidelity to what each day brings.
A. E. Dunning

The sure way to miss success is to miss the opportunity.
Victor Chasles

Opportunity, sooner or later, comes to all who work and wish.
Lord Stanley

When one door closes another opens. But often we look so long so regretfully upon the closed door that we fail to see the one that has opened for us.
Helen Keller

Take all the swift advantage of the hours.
William Shakespeare

Opportunities do not come with their values stamped upon them. Everyone must be challenged. A day dawns, quite like other days; in it a single hour comes, quite like other hours; but in that day and in that hour the chance of a lifetime faces us.
Maltbie Davenport Babcock

Many do with opportunities as children do at the seashore; they fill their little hands with sand, and then let the grains fall through, one by one.
Thomas Jones

The future is an opportunity.
J. F. Ware

The race is not to the swift or the battle to the strong, nor does food come to the wise or wealth to the brilliant or favor to the learned; but time and chance happen to them all.
Ecclesiastes 9:11

To improve the golden moment of opportunity, and catch the good that is within our reach, is the great art of life.
Samuel Johnson

Opportunities are on every hand; what we need is, not a new chance, but clearness of vision to discern the chance which at this very hour is ours, if we recognize it.
Katherine Krieger

A man in earnest finds means or, if he cannot find, creates them.
William Ellery Channing

Take time to deliberate; but when the time for action arrives, stop thinking and go in.
Andrew Jackson

Who seeks, and will not take, when once 'tis offered, Shall never find it more.
William Shakespeare

And then one day you find ten years have got behind you. No one told you when to run, you missed the starting gun.
Time lyrics, Pink Floyd

When the time comes in which one could, the time has passed in which one can.
Marie Ebner Eschenbach

There's a time for all things.
William Shakespeare

The golden moments in the stream of life rush past us, and we see nothing but sand; the angels come to visit us, and we only know them when they are gone.
George Eliot

We have the power within, but the secret of success is to employ our power and talents and be prepared for opportunity when it comes.
Walter Matthews

We must look for the opportunity in every difficulty instead of being paralyzed at the thought of the difficulty in every opportunity.
Walter E. Cole

A good opportunity is seldom presented, and is easily lost.
Syrus

The secret of success in life is for a man to be ready for his opportunity when it comes.
Benjamin Disraeli

You will never "find" time for anything. If you want time, you must make it.
Charles Buxton

Who cannot but see oftentimes how strange the threads of our destiny run? Oft it is only for a moment the favourable instant is presented. We miss it, and months and years are lost.
Ludwig Tieck

How often events, by chance, and unexpectedly, came to pass, which you had not dared even to hope for!
Terence

Present opportunities are not to be neglected; they rarely visit us twice.
Voltaire

Arrange whatever pieces come your way.
Virginia Woolf

Do not wait for ideal circumstances, nor for the best
opportunities; they will never come.
Janet Erskine Stuart

Occasions are rare: and those who know how to seize upon them
are rarer.
H. W. Shaw

Luck affects everything. Let your hook always be cast. In the
stream where you least expect it, there will be a fish.
Ovid

The greatest achievement of the human spirit is to live up to
one's opportunities and make the most of one's resources.
Marquis de Vauvenargues

Chance is always powerful; let your hook always be cast in a pool
where you least expect there will be fish.
Ovid

How often events, by chance and unexpectedly, come to pass,
which you had not dared even to hope for!
Terence

A stray, unthought-of five minutes may contain the event of a
life, and this all-important moment — who can tell when it will
be upon us?
Dean Alford

Opportunity is rare, and a wise man will never let it go by him.
Bayard Taylor

Do not suppose opportunity will knock twice at your door.
Nicolas de Chamfort

Improve time in the present; for opportunity is precious, and time is a sword.
Saadi

Great quotes on Character Building

You cannot dream yourself into a character; you must hammer and forge yourself one.
Henry David Thoreau

Be your character what it will, it will be known, and nobody will take it upon your word.
Lord Chesterfield

Reputation is what men and women think of us; character is what God and angels know of us.
Thomas Paine

Nothing of character is really permanent but virtue and personal worth.
Daniel Webster

The essential thing is not knowledge, but character.
Joseph Le Conte

It requires less character to discover the faults of others, than to tolerate them.
J. Petit Senn

A good name will shine forever.
Proverb

A fair reputation is a plant, delicate in its nature, and by no means rapid in its growth. It will not shoot up in a night like the gourd of the prophet; but, like that gourd, it may perish in a night.
Jeremy Taylor

Sow an act, and you reap a habit; sow a habit, and you reap a character; sow a character, and you reap a destiny.
George Dana Boardman

Talents are best nurtured in solitude. Character is best formed in the stormy billows of the world.
Johann Wolfgang Von Goethe

Our character is but the stamp on our souls of the free choices of good and evil we have made through life.
John C. Geikie

Reputation is for time; character is for eternity.
J. B. Gough

Character is a diamond that scratches every other stone.
Cyrus A. Bartol

In the stormy current of life characters are weights or floats, which at one time make us glide along the bottom, and at another, maintain us on the surface.
Hippolyte Taine

Nature magically suits a man to his fortunes, by making them the fruit of his character.
Ralph Waldo Emerson

Talents are best nurtured in solitude, but character is best formed in the stormy billows of the world.
Johann Wolfgang von Goethe

Characters do not change. Opinions alter, but characters are only developed.
Benjamin Disraeli

A man's character is like his shadow, which sometimes follows and sometimes precedes him, and which is occasionally longer, occasionally shorter, than he is.
Madame de la Rochejuquelein

Men best show their character in trifles, where they are not on their guard. It is in the simplest habits, that we often see the boundless egotism which pays no regard to the feelings of others and denies nothing to itself.
Arthur Schopenhauer

Every man, as to character, is the creature of the age in which he lives. Very few are able to raise themselves above the ideas of their times.
Voltaire

It is of little traits that the greatest human character is composed.
William Winter

Character and personal force are the only investments that are worth anything.
Walt Whitman

You must be the change you wish to see in the world.
Mahatma Ghandi

Character lives in a man, reputation outside of him.
J. G. Holland

There comes a time when one must take a position that is neither safe, nor politic, nor popular, but he must take it because his conscience tells him it is right.
Martin Luther

Take time to deliberate; but when the time for action arrives, stop thinking and go in.
Andrew Jackson

Character is, for the most part,
simply habit become fixed.
C. H. Parkhurst

We are builders of our own characters. We have different positions, spheres, capacities, privileges, different work to do in the world, different temporal fabrics to raise; but we are all alike in this, -- all are architects of fate.
John Fothergill Waterhouse Ware

Character is, in the long run, the decisive factor in the life of individuals and of nations alike.
Theodore Roosevelt

Actions, looks, words and steps form the alphabet by which you may spell character.
Johann Kasper Lavater

Every human being is intended to have a character of his own; to be what no others are, and to do what no other can do.
William Henry Channing

Let us not say, Every man is the architect of his own fortune; but let us say, Every man is the architect of his own character.
George Dana Boardman

Fate is character.
William Winter

Character is higher than intellect. A great soul will be strong to live, as well as strong to think.
Ralph Waldo Emerson

Such as are thy habitual thoughts, such also will be the character of thy mind; for the soul is dyed by the thoughts.
Marcus Aurelius

Great quotes on Destiny

You are what your deep, driving desire is.
As your desire is, so is your will.
As your will is, so is your deed.
As your deed is, so is your destiny.
Brihadaranyaka Upanishad IV 4.5

If we would see the color of our future, we must look for it in our present; if we would gaze on the star of our destiny, we must look for it in our hearts.
Canon Farrar

Everywhere man blames nature and fate, yet his fate is mostly but the echo of his character and passions, his mistakes and weaknesses.
Democritus

Love nothing but that which comes to you woven in the pattern of your destiny. For what could more aptly fit your needs?
Marcus Aurelius

It is a mistake to look too far ahead. Only one link of the chain of destiny can be handled at a time.
Winston Churchill

Adapt yourself to the life you have been given; and truly love the people with whom destiny has surrounded you.
Marcus Aurelius

Happy is the man who can do only one thing; in doing it, he fulfills his destiny.
Joseph Joubert

Let us follow our destiny, ebb and flow. Whatever may happen, we master fortune by accepting it.
Virgil

The future depends on what we do in the present.
Mahatma Gandhi

If you don't know where you are going, you'll end up some place
else.
Yogi Berra

The destiny of man is in his own soul.
Herodotus

Where do we go on this road which we have followed for so long
without ever asking: where does it lead us?
Lanza del Vasto

Our destiny can be examined, but it cannot be justified or totally
explained. We are simply here.
Iris Murdoch

The acts of this life are the destiny of the next. He hath no leisure
who uses it not. He that will not reflect is a ruined man.
Eastern Proverb

Every man has his own destiny; the only imperative is to follow
it, to accept it, no matter where it leads him.
Henry Miller

The tissue of life to be we weave with colors all our own,
And in the field of destiny we reap as we have sown.
John Greenleaf Whittier

There is a divinity that shapes our ends, Rough-hew them how
we will.
William Shakespeare

Our destiny changes with our thoughts; we shall become what
we wish to become, do what we wish to do, when our habitual
thoughts correspond with our desires.
Orison Swett Marden

A man's happiness or unhappiness depends as much on his temperament as on his destiny.
Francois de La Rochefoucauld

Destiny is not a matter of chance; but a matter of choice. It is not a thing to be waited for, It is a thing to be acheived.
William Jennings Bryan

Character is destiny.
Heraclitus

All the world is a stage and all the men and women are merely players: each have their part
William Shakespeare

Great quotes on History

The disadvantage of men not knowing the past is that they do not know the present. History is a hill or high point of vantage, from which alone men see the town in which they live or the age in which they are living.
G. K. Chesterson

We need history, not to tell us what happened or to explain the past, but to make the past alive so that it can explain us and make a future possible.
Alan Bloom

A good writer of history is a guy who is suspicious.
Jon Bishop

To be ignorant of what occurred before you were born is to remain always a child. For what is the worth of human life, unless it is woven into the life of our ancestors by the records of history?
Cicero

The history of the world is none other than progress of the consciousness of freedom.
George Hegel

The time for extracting a lesson from history is ever at hand for those who are wise.
Desmosthenes

History is a mighty drama, enacted upon the theatre of time, with suns for lamps, and eternity for a background.
Thomas Carlyle

To have a sense of history one must consider oneself a piece of history.
Alfred Kazin

History is not, of course, a cookbook offering pretested recipes. It teaches by analogy, not by maxims.
Henry Kissinger

History is philosophy learned from examples.
Dionysius

Our clock strikes when there is a change from hour to hour; but no hammer in the Horologe of Time peals through the universe when there is a change from era to era.
Thomas Carlyle

Every great writer is a writer of history, let him treat on what subject he may.— He carries with lmn. for thousands of years, a portion of his times.
Walter Savage Landor

Life can only be understood backwards, but it must be lived forwards.
Soren Kierkegaard

A historian is a prophet in reverse.
Friedrich von Schlegel

In spite of the recent triumphs of science, men haven't changed much in the last 2,000 years, and in consequence, we must still try to learn from history. History is ourselves.
Kenneth Clark

Perhaps, one day, remembering even these things will bring pleasure.
(*Forsan et haec olim meminisse iuvabit*)
Virgil

Great quotes on Nature

Nature is a self-made machine, more perfectly automated than any automated machine. To create something in the image of nature is to create a machine, and it was by learning the inner working of nature that man became a builder of machines.
Eric Hoffer

He that plants trees loves others beside himself.
Thomas Fuller

Woodman spare that tree!
Touch not a single bough!
In youth it sheltered me,
And I'll protect it now.
George Pope Morris

Come forth into the light of things
Let nature be your teacher.
William Wordsworth

The chessboard is the world, the pieces are the phenomena of the universe, the rules of the game are what we call the laws of Nature, the players on the other side is hidden from us.
Thomas Henry Huxley

When one tugs at a single thing in nature, he finds it attached to the rest of the world.
John Muir

How I do love the earth. I feel it thrill under my feet. I feel somehow as if it were conscious of my love, as if something passed into my dancing blood from it.
James Russell Lowell

When we plant a tree, we are doing what we can to make our
planet a more wholesome and happier dwelling place for those
who come after us, if not for ourselves.
Oliver Wendell Holmes

Civilization exists by geological consent,
subject to change without notice.
Will Durant

The Amen! of Nature is always a flower.
Oliver Wendall Holmes

But mighty Nature bounds as from her birth;
The sun is in the heavens, and life on earth:
Flowers in the valley, splendor in the beam,
Health on the gale, and freshness in the stream.
Lord Byron

All Nature wears one universal grin.
Henry Fielding

To the wisest man, wide as is his vision. Nature remains of quite
infinite depth, of quite infinite expansion and all experience
thereof limits itself to some few computed centuries and
measured square miles.
Thomas Carlyle

You will find something far greater in the woods than you will
find in books. Stones and trees will teach you that which you will
never learn from masters.
St. Bernard

The sky is the daily bread of the eyes.
Ralph Waldo Emerson

Nature is an endless combination and repetition of a very few
laws.
Ralph Waldo Emerson

Come forth into the light of things,
Let Nature be your teacher.
William Wordsworth

In all things of nature there is something of the marvelous.
Aristotle

The wind, a sightless laborer, whistles at his task.
William Wordsworth

The laws of nature are written deep in the folds and faults of the
earth. By encouraging men to learn those laws one can lead them
further to a knowledge of the author of all laws.
John Joseph Lynch

Great quotes on Food and Cooking

Hunger is the best sauce in the world.
Cervantes

Strange to see how a good dinner and
feasting reconciles everybody.
Samuel Pepys

A good cook is the peculiar gift of the gods. He must be a perfect
creature from the brain to the palate, from the palate to the
finger's end.
Walter Savage Landor

Kissing don't last: cookery do.
George Meredith

Cooking is like love. It should be entered into with abandon or
not at all.
Harriet Van Horne

Savory seasonings stimulate the appetite.
Latin Proverb

Fish, to taste right, must swim three times -- in water, in butter
and in wine.
Polish Proverb

Man is what he eats.
German Proverb

Hunger finds no fault with the cooking.
Proverb

A good meal makes a man feel more charitable toward the world
than any sermon.
Arthur Pendenys

Fervet olla, vivit amicitia: While the pot boils, friendship endures. (Meaning the man who gives good dinners has plenty of friends).
Latin Proverb

Cookery has become a noble art, a noble science; cooks are gentlemen.
Robert Burton

The discovery of a new dish does more for the happiness of mankind than the discovery of a star.
Anthelme Brillat-Savarin

A hungry stomach seldoms scorns plain food.
Horace

I feel a recipe is only a theme, which an intelligent cook can play each time with a variation.
Madam Benoit

Even were a cook to cook a fly,
he would keep the breast for himself.
Polish Proverb

Great quotes on Thoughts & Thinking

It is good to rub and polish our brains against that of others.
Michel de Montaigne

We think too small. Like the frog at the bottom of the well. He thinks the sky is only as big as the top of the well. If he surfaced, he would have an entirely different view.
Mao Tse-Tung

Where all think alike, no one thinks very much.
Walter Lipman

Thoughts are but dreams till their effects be tried.
William Shakespeare

Words without thoughts never to heaven go.
William Shakespeare

Nurture your mind with great thoughts. To believe in the heroic makes heroes.
Benjamin Disraeli

Men give me some credit for genius. All the genius I have lies in this: When I have a subject in hand, I study it profoundly. Day and night it is before me. I explore it in all its bearings. My mind becomes pervaded with it. Then the effort which I make is what the people call the fruit of genius. It is the fruit of labor and thought.
Alexander Hamilton

The aim of education should be to teach us how to think, rather than what to think.
James Beattie

What gems of painting or statuary are in the world of art, or what flowers are in the world of nature, are gems of thought to the cultivated and the thinking.
Oliver Wendell Holmes

We bring forth weeds when our quick minds lie still.
William Shakespeare

All truly wise thoughts have been thought already, thousands of times; but to make them truly ours, we must think them over again honestly, till they take firm root in our personal experience.
Johann Wolfgang von Goethe

The less men think, the more they talk.
Baron Montesquieu

Learning without thought is labor lost; thought without learning is perilous.
Confucius

The universe is change;
our life is what our thoughts make it.
Marcus Aurelius

But words are things, and a small drop of ink
Falling like dew upon a thought, produces
That which makes thousands, perhaps millions, think.
Sir Aubrey De Vere

Thoughts rule the world.
Ralph Waldo Emerson

Thinking is the talking of the soul with itself.
Plato

Impromptu thoughts are mental wild-flowers.
Mme. du Deffand

Your disposition will be suitable to that which you most frequently think on; for the soul is, as it were, tinged with the colour and complexion of its own thoughts.
Marcus Antonius

Thinking is the hardest work there is, which is the probably reason why so few people engage in it.
Henry Ford

What I must do is all that concerns me, not what other people think.
Ralph Waldo Emerson

The efficient man is the man who thinks for himself, and is capable of thinking hard and long.
Charles W. Eliot

They are never alone that are accompanied with noble thoughts.
Sir Philip Sidney

Change your thoughts and you change your world.
Norman Vincent Peale

Obvious thinking commonly leads to wrong judgments and wrong conclusions.
Humphrey B. Neil

Language is the close-fitting dress of thought.
R. C. Trench

To live is to think.
Cicero

Great quotes on Self Development

The way to gain a good reputation, is to endeavor to be what you desire to appear. - Socrates

The fact is, that to do anything in the world worth doing, we must not stand back shivering and thinking of the cold and danger, but jump in and scramble through as well as we can.
Robert Cushing

The searching-out and thorough investigation of truth ought to be the primary study of man.
Cicero

The only journey is the journey within.
Rainer Maria Rilke

Know thyself means this, that you get acquainted with what you know, and what you can do.
Menander

Yes, know thyself: in great concerns or small,
Be this thy care, for this, my friend, is all.
Juvenal

Men soon the faults of others learn
A few their virtues, too, find out;
But is there one—I have a doubt—
Who can his own defects discern?
Sanskrit Proverb

Collect as precious pearls the words of the wise and virtuous.
Abd-el-Kadar

If we do not plant knowledge when young, it will give us no shade when we are old.
Lord Chesterfield

If you have an hour, will you not improve that hour, instead of idling it away?
Lord Chesterfield

When I want to read a novel, I write one.
Benjamin Disraeli

If we are facing in the right direction, all we have to do is keep on walking.
Zen Proverb

In questions of science, the authority of a thousand is not worth the humble reasoning of a single individual.
Galileo Galilei

Follow your honest convictions, and stay strong.
William Thackeray

The most difficult thing in life is to know yourself.
Thales

He that will not reflect is a ruined man.
Asian Proverb

Every day do something that will inch you closer to a better tomorrow.
Doug Firebaugh

Be not afraid of growing slowly; be afraid only of standing still.
Chinese Proverb

God ever works with those who work with will.
Aeschylus

Insist on yourself. Never imitate.
Ralph Waldo Emerson

Heaven never helps the man who will not act.
Sophocles

If you don't know where you are going,
You will end up some place else.
Yogi Berra

Knowing yourself is the beginning of all wisdom.
Aristotle

Our ideas, like orange-plants, spread out in proportion to the
size of the box, which imprisons the roots.
Edward Bulwer Lytton

We are sometimes as different from ourselves as we are from
others.
Francois de La Rochefoucauld

In learning to know other things, and other minds, we become
more intimately acquainted with ourselves, and are to ourselves
better worth knowing.
Philip Gilbert Hamilton

What progress, you ask, have I made? I have begun to be a friend
to myself.
Hecato, Greek philosopher

We are either progressing or retrograding all the while; there is
no such thing as remaining stationary in this life.
James Freeman Clarke

To conquer oneself is the best and noblest victory; to be
vanquished by one's own nature is the worst and most ignoble
defeat.
Plato

Everybody wants to be somebody;
nobody wants to grow.
Johann Wolfgang von Goethe

The happiest life is that which constantly exercises and educates
what is best in us.
Hamerton

We only become what we are by the radical and deep-seated
refusal of that which others have made of us.
Jean-Paul Sartre

Change and growth take place when a person has risked himself
and dares to become involved with experimenting with his own
life.
Herbert Otto

Heed the still small voice that so seldom leads us wrong, and
never into folly.
Marquise du Deffand

Your real influence is measured by your treatment of yourself.
A. Bronson Alcott

Energy and persistence conquer all things.
Benjamin Franklin

If we all did the things we are capable of,
we would astound ourselves.
Thomas Edison

A man who finds no satisfaction in himself will seek for it in vain
elsewhere.
La Rochefoucauld

Fear less, hope more, eat less, chew more, whine less, breathe more, talk less, say more, hate less, love more, and good things will be yours.
Swedish Proverb

Make it thy business to know thyself, which is the most difficult lesson in the world.
Miguel de Cervantes

The best rules to form a young man are: to talk little, to hear much, to reflect alone upon what has passed in company, to distrust one's own opinions, and value others that deserve it.
Sir William Temple

Exert your talents, and distinguish yourself, and don't think of retiring from the world, until the world will be sorry that you retire.
Samuel Johnson

Great quotes on Fear of Failure

Go back a little to leap further.
John Clarke

The fact is that in order to do any thing in this world worth
doing, we must not stand shivering on the bank thinking of the
cold and the danger, but jump in and scramble through as well as
we can.
Sydney Smith

It is hard to fail, but it is worse never to have tried to succeed.
Theodore Roosevelt

Half of the failures in life come from pulling one's horse when he
is leaping.
Thomas Hood

I failed my way to success.
Thomas Edison

If we all worked on the assumption that what is accepted as true
were really true,
there would be little hope of advance.
Orville Wright

Our doubts are traitors, and make us lose the good we oft might
win, by fearing to attempt.
William Shakespeare

Every failure brings with it the seed of an equivalent success.
Napoleon Hill

Failure is blindness to the strategic element in events; success is
readiness for instant action when the opportune moment
arrives.
Newell D. Hillis

They fail, and they alone, who have not striven.
Thomas Bailey Aldrich

We learn wisdom from failure much more than success. We often discover what we will do, by finding out what we will not do.
Samuel Smiles

I was never afraid of failure, for I would sooner fail than not be among the best.
John Keats

It is foolish to fear what you cannot avoid.
Stultum est timere quod vitare non potes.
Publius Syrus

He that is down needs fear no fall.
John Bunyan

Never let the fear of striking out get in your way.
George Herman "Babe" Ruth

One who fears failure limits his activities.
Failure is only the opportunity to more
intelligently begin again.
Henry Ford

The greatest mistake you can make in life is to continually be afraid you will make one.
Elbert Hubbard

Little minds are tamed and subdued by misfortunes; but great minds rise above them.
Washington Irving

Our greatest glory consist not in never falling, but in rising every time we fall.
Oliver Goldsmith

Wherever we look upon this earth, the opportunities take shape within the problems.
Nelson A. Rockefeller

What would life be if we had no courage to attempt anything?
Vincent van Gogh

The greatest men sometimes overshoot themselves, but then their very mistakes are so many lessons of instruction.
Tom Browne

Experience teaches slowly, and at the cost of mistakes.
James A. Froude

It is the want of diligence, rather than the want of means, that causes most failures.
Alfred Mercier

It is stupidity to fear what you cannot avoid.
(*Stultum est timere quod vitare non potes*)
Publius Syrus

A man's life is interesting primarily when he has failed, I well know, for it's a sign that he tried to surpass himself.
Georges Clemenceau

He who fears being conquered is sure of defeat.
Napoleon Bonaparte

No one can give something he does not have.
(*Nemo dat quod non habet*)
Cicero

Not failure, but low aim, is crime.
James Russell Lowell

There is no failure except in no longer trying.
Elbert Hubbard

There is no impossibility to him who stands prepared to conquer every hazard.
The fearful are the failing.
Sarah J. Hale

Anyone who has never made a mistake
has never tried anything new.
Albert Einstein

Disappointments are to the soul what thunderstorms are to the air.
Johann C. F. von Schiller

Failure teaches success.
Japanese Saying

The one who feared he could not, sat on his hands.
(*Sedit qui timuit, ne non succederet*)
Gaius Julius Caesar

Great quotes on Experience

Experience is a grindstone; and it is lucky for us, if we can get brightened by it, and not ground.
Josh Billings

Experience is by industry achieved, And perfected by the swift course of time.
William Shakespeare

Experience keeps a dear school, but fools will learn in no other, and scarce in that; for it is true we may give advice, but we cannot give conduct.
Benjamin Franklin

The education of circumstances is superior to that of tuition.
William Wordsworth

It is good to learn what to avoid by studying the misfortunes of others.
Publius Syrius

The experience of others adds to our knowledge, but not to our wisdom; that is dearer bought.
Hosea Ballou

All truly wise thoughts have been thought already, thousands of times; but to make them truly ours, we must think them over again honestly, until they take firm root in our personal experience.
Johann Wolfgang von Goethe

He knows the water best that has waded through it.
Danish Proverb

If you would know the road ahead, ask someone who has traveled it.
Chinese Proverb

Experience is by industry achieved
And perfected by the swift course of time.
William Shakespeare

The years teach much which the days never know.
Ralph Waldo Emerson

Those who come last enter with advantage.— They are born to
the wealth of antiquity.— The materials for judging are
prepared, and the foundations of knowledge are laid to their
hands.—Besides, if the point was tried by antiquity, antiquity
would lose it, for the present age is really the oldest, and has the
largest experience to plead.
Collier

All experience is an arch to build upon.
Henry Brook Adams

Experience is a jewel, and it had need be so, for it is often
purchased at an infinite rate.
William Shakespeare

Experience is a safe light to walk by, and he is not a rash man
who expects to succeed in future from the same means which
have secured it in times past.
Wendell Phillips

Pick up a grain a day and add to your heap. You will soon learn,
by happy experience, the power of littles as applied to
intellectual processes and gains.
John S. Hart

That learning which thou gettest by thy own observation and
experience, is far beyond that which thou gettest by precept; as
the knowledge of a traveler exceeds that which is got by reading.
Thomas à Kempis

A moment's insight is sometimes worth a life's experience.
Oliver Wendall Holmes

Experience is not what happens to a man: it is what a man does
with what happens to him.
Aldous Huxley

Experience is the universal mother of sciences.
Miguel de Cervantes

Experience is the child of thought, and thought is the child of
action. We cannot learn men from books.
Benjamin Disraeli

Experience does not err; only your judgments err by expecting
from her what is not in her power.
Lenoardo da Vinci

We learn by experience.
(*Experientia docuit.*)
Tacitus

Great quotes on Worrying and Hope

Don't waste your life in doubts and fears: spend yourself on the work before you, well assured that the right performance of this hour's duties will be the best preparation for the hours or ages that follow it.
Ralph Waldo Emerson

No longer forward nor behind
I look in hope and fear;
But grateful take the good I find,
The best of now and here.
John G. Whittier

It is not work that kills men, it is worry. Work is healthy; you can hardly put more on a man than he can bear. But worry is rust upon the blade. It is not movement that destroys the machinery, but friction.
Henry Ward Beecher

Be just, and fear not.
Let all the ends thou aim'st at be thy country's,
Thy God's and truth's.
William Shakespeare

Man is not the creature of circumstances. Circumstances are the creatures of man.
Benjamin Disraeli

You have enemies? Good. That means you've stood up for something, sometime in your life
Winston Churchill

Never let life's hardships disturb you ... no one can avoid problems, not even saints or sages.
Nichiren Daishonen

Ask yourself this question:
"Will this matter a year from now?"
Richard Carlson, writing in Don't Sweat the Small Stuff

Surely there is something in the unruffled calm of nature that overawes our little anxieties and doubts; the sight of the deep-blue sky and the clustering stars above seems to impart a quiet to the mind.
Jonathan Edwards

Do not anticipate trouble, or worry about what may never happen. Keep in the sunlight.
Benjamin Franklin

Imagine every day to be the last of a life surrounded with hopes, cares, anger and fear. The hours that come unexpectedly will be much the more grateful.
Horace

The mind that is anxious about future events is miserable.
Seneca

Present fears are less than horrible imaginings.
William Shakespeare

We always strive after what is forbidden, and desire the things refused us.
Ovid

Let us be of good cheer, remembering that the misfortunes hardest to bear are those that never happen.
James Russel Lowell

How much pain have cost us the evils that have never happened.
Thomas Jefferson

It is the trouble that never comes that causes the loss of sleep.
Chas. Austin Bates

Nothing can bring you peace but yourself.
Ralph Waldo Emerson

Live in each season as it passes; breathe the air, drink the drink,
taste the fruit, and resign yourself to the influences of each.
Henry David Thoreau

We also deem those happy, who from the experience of life, have
learned to bear its ills and without descanting on their weight.
Junvenal

Thus each person by his fears gives wings to rumor, and, without
any real source of apprehension, men fear what they themselves
have imagined.
Lucan

I never think of the future - it comes soon enough.
Albert Einstein

That which does not kill you makes you stronger.
Neitzsche

It is better to light one candle than to curse the darkness.
Chinese Proverb

It is idle to dread what you cannot avoid.
Publius Syrus

He either fears his fate too much,
Or his deserts are small,
Who dares not put it to the touch
To gain or lose it all.
Marquis of Montrose

The rose is fairest when 't is budding new,
and hope is brightest when it dawns from fears.
Walter Scott

The first and greatest commandment is,
Don't let them scare you.
Elmer Davis

My life has been full of terrible misfortunes most of which never
happened.
Michel de Montaigne

Great quotes on Friendship

Value friendship for what there is in it,
not for what can be gotten out of it.
H. Clay Trumbull

Friends are like melons. Shall I tell you why?
To find a good one, you must a hundred try.
Claude Mermet

One friend in a lifetime is much; two are many;
three are hardly possible.
Henry Adams

Friendship is the soul's heaven.
A. Bronson Alcott

A friend is, as it were, a second self.
Cicero

Be gracious to all men, but choose the best to be your friends.
Isocrates

Friendship needs no words--it is solitude delivered from the
anguish of loneliness.
Dag Hammarskjold

A friend is one who dislikes the same people you dislike.
Unknown

Sincerity, truth, faithfulness, come into the very essence of
friendship.
William Ellery

There is no surer bond of friendship than an identity of
community of ideas and tastes.
Cicero

We should behave to our friends as we would wish our friends behave to us.
Aristotle

Friendship, like phosphorus, shines brightest when all around is dark.
Proverb

Friends are like melons. You may try fifty before you find a good one.
Claude Mermet

Have friends. 'Tis a second existence.
Baltasar Gracian

Difference of opinion was never, with me, a motive of separation from a friend.
Thomas Jefferson

A friend in need is a friend indeed;
A friend who bleeds is better.
Placebo – "Pure Morning"

Reprove your friends in secret, praise them openly.
Publilius Syrus

A good deed is never lost: he who sows courtesy reaps friendship; and he who plants kindness, gathers love.
Basil

I keep my friends as misers do their treasure,
because, of all the things granted us by wisdom,
none is greater or better than friendship.
Pietro Aretino

You will make more friends in a week by getting yourself interested in other people than you can in a year by trying to get people interested in you.
Arnold Bennett

Let friendship creep gently to a height; if it rush to it, it may soon run itself out of breath.
Thomas Fuller

True friendship's laws are by this rule express'd.
Welcome the coming, speed the parting guest.
Alexander Pope

In prosperity it is very easy to find a friend;
in adversity, nothing is so difficult.
Epictetus

If a man does not make new acquaintances as he passes through life, he will soon find himself alone. A man should keep his friendships in constant repair.
Samuel Johnson

Make not thy friend to cheap to thee,
nor thyself to thy friend.
Thomas Fuller

Wishing to be friends is quick work,
but friendship is a slow ripening fruit.
Aristotle

Friendship makes prosperity more brilliant,
and lightens adversity by dividing and sharing it.
Cicero

Hold a true friend with both your hands.
Nigerian Proverb

Tell me your friends, and I'll tell you who you are.
Assyrian Proverb

The proper office of a friend is to side with you when you are in the wrong. Nearly anybody will side with you when you are in the right.
Mark Twain

Go often to the house of thy friend,
for weeds choke the unused path.
Ralph Waldo Emerson

Great quotes on Love

There are three things that last: faith, hope and love, and the greatest of these is love.
I Corinthians 13:13

Hear the mellow wedding bells Golden bells!
What a world of happiness their harmony foretells
Through the balmy air of night
How they ring out their delight!
Edgar Alan Poe

Here's to the bride and the bridegroom
We'll ask their success in our prayers
And through life's dark shadows and sunshine
That good luck may always be theirs.
Armenian Toast

May your eyes stay filled with stars and your hearts with visions of dreams yet to come.
Traditional Wedding Toast

Come live with me and be my love,
And we will some new pleasures prove
Of golden sands, and crystal books
With silken lines, and silver books.
John Donne

Now you will feel no rain, for each of you will be the shelter for the other. Now you will feel no cold, for each of you will be the warmth to the other. Now you are two persons, but there is only one life before you. Go now to your dwelling, to enter into the days of your life together, and may your days be good and long upon the earth.
Apache Blessing

Marriage is love personified.
Phoenix Flame

Blest is the bride on whom the sun doth shine.
Iris Murdoch

The ideal that marriage aims at is that of spiritual union through the physical. The human love that it incarnates is intended to serve as a stepping stone to divine or universal love.
Mohandas K. Gandhi

Great quotes on Wealth and Money

Money can't buy everything--for example poverty.
Nelson Algren

Soon gotten, soon spent; ill gotten, ill spent.
John Heywood

A man's true wealth is the good he does in this world.
Bendixline

Wealth consists not in having great possessions but in having few wants.
Epicurus

If you know how to spend less than you get, you have the philosopher's stone.
Benjamin Franklin
from Quotations About Spending Money

I want the whole of Europe to have one currency; it will make trading much easier.
Napoleon I

Men do not understand how great a revenue is economy.
Cicero

Poverty is a blessing hated by all men.
Italian Proverb

If your riches are yours, why don't you take them with you to t'other world?
Ben Franklin

The almighty dollar, that great object of universal devotion throughout our land.
Washington Irving

Money alone sets all the world in motion.
Publius Syrus

Put not your trust in money,
but put your money in trust.
Oliver Wendell Holmes

If money go before, all ways do lie open.
William Shakespeare, The Merry Wives of Windsor

Money amassed either serves us or rules us.
Horace

Money talks, but all it ever says is good-bye.
American Proverb

A full purse is not as good as an empty one is bad.
Yiddish Proverb

Great quotes on Quotes and Proverbs

One must be a wise reader to quote wisely and well.
Amos Bronson Alcott

The maxims of men disclose their hearts.
French Proverb

To select well among old things, is almost equal to inventing new ones.
 Nicholas Charles Trublet

I have gathered a posie of other men's flowers, and nothing but the thread that binds them is my own.
Michel de Montaigne

Proverbs are mental gems gathered in the diamond districts of the mind.
William R. Alger

What gems of painting or statuary are in the world of art, or what flowers are in the world of nature, are gems of thought to the cultivated and the thinking.
Oliver Wendell Holmes

Stealing someone else's words frequently spares the embarrassment of eating your own.
Peter Anderson

A short saying oft contains much wisdom.
Sophocles

It often happens that the quotations constitute the most valuable part of a book.
Vicesimus Knox

A collection of rare thoughts is nothing less than a cabinet of intellectual gems.
William B. Sprague

Good sayings are like pearls strung together.
Chinese Proverb

A proverb is to speech what salt is to food.
Arabic Proverb

Proverbs are the cream of a nation's thought.
Unknown

There is not less wit, not less invention, in applying rightly a thought one finds in a book, than in being the first author of that book.
Pierre Boyle

A proverb is much matter decocted into few words.
Thomas Fuller

A maxim is the exact and noble expression of an important and indisputable truth. Good maxims are the germs of all excellence; when firmly fixed on the memory, they nourish the will.
Joseph Joubert

Nothing gives an author so much pleasure as to find his works respectfully quoted by other learned authors.
Benjamin Franklin

It is delightful to transport one's self into the spirit of the past, to see how a wise man has thought before us, and to what glorious height we have at last reached. Johann Wolfgang von Goethe

Time is of of no account with great thoughts, which are as fresh today as when they first passed through their authors' minds ages ago.
Samuel Smiles

The diamond may adorn royalty, regardless of personal worth; but jewels of thought render even poverty illustrious and sublime.
- found in Gems for the Fireside

Proverbs may be said to be the abridgment of wisdom.
Joseph Joubert

The proverb answers where the sermon fails.
W. G. Simms

Human success is a quotation from overhead.
Charles H. Parkhurst

A well-cultivated mind is, so to speak, made up of all the minds of preceding ages; it is only one single mind which has been educated during all this time. Bernard de Bovier de Fontenelle

Maxims are the condensed good sense of nations.
Sir J. Mackintosh

A proverb is a wise saying, old yet radiant with novelty.
Erasmus

Many ideas grow better when transplanted into another mind, than in the one where they sprung up.
Oliver Wendell Holmes

Always have a book at hand, in the parlor, on the table, for the family; a book of condensed thought and striking anecdote, of sound maxims and truthful apothegms. It will impress on your own mind a thousand valuable suggestions, and teach your children a thousand lessons of truth and duty. Such a book is a casket of jewels for your household.
Tryon Edwards

When I quote others I do so in order to express my own ideas more clearly.
Michel de Montaigne